Nell and T

Written by Rachel Russ

Illustrated by Elif Balta Parks

Collins

Nell picks a cat hat.

Tess picks a cat hat.

Tess packs a red bag.

Nell packs a red bag.

Nell has a big bell.

Tess has no big bell.

Tess gets off and tuts.

Nell huffs and puffs.

Tess is up a hill.

Tess is in a mess.

Nell can get Tess up.

Nell is in a mess!

🐾 Review: After reading 🐾

Use your assessment from hearing the children read to choose any GPCs, words or tricky words that need additional practice.

Read 1: Decoding
- Ask the children to sound talk and blend each of the following words: h/u/ff, m/e/ss, p/a/ck/s, p/i/ck/s.
- Can you match the rhyming words? **bell**, **Tess**, **huffs**, **puffs**, **Nell**, **mess**. (*bell/Nell, Tess/mess, huff/puff*)
- Look at the "I spy sounds" pages (14–15). Discuss the picture with the children. Can they find items/ examples of words with the /l/ and "ll" sounds? (*lion, laugh, leaf, leaves, lemon, lemonade, log, lock, doll, roll, fill, ball*)

Read 2: Prosody
- Choose two double page spreads and model reading with expression to the children. Ask the children to have a go at reading the same pages with expression.
- Reread the whole book to the children to model fluency and rhythm in the story.

Read 3: Comprehension
- For every question ask the children how they know the answer. Ask:
  o Do you like doing the same things as your friends?
  o What type of hats do Tess and Nell pick? (*cat hats*) Why do you think they are called cat hats? (*because they have ears like cats*)
  o What is different about Tess and Nell's scooters? (*Nell has a bell and Tess doesn't have a bell*)
  o How are Tess and Nell feeling on pages 8 and 9? How do you know? (e.g. *they are cross/angry/upset with each other. We can tell because they are walking away/they are making the sounds "huff", "puff" and "tut". They have annoyed expressions on their faces*)
  o Can you explain why Tess and Nell have an argument? (*because their scooters do not match*)
  o How do Nell and Tess make friends again? (*Nell helps Tess out of the mud*)